Carol —

It is a pleasure
for me to autograph this
book for you. My he.
you will enjoy reading
enjoyed all the years we had
at the bank.

best wishes,
Bill McLaughlin 2008

MW00718035

Beyond The Mountain

The Climb is Challenging
The Valley is Beautiful

bill mclaughlin

Waldenhouse Publishers, Inc.
Walden, Tennessee

Beyond ^{The}Mountain: The Climb is Challenging; The Valley is Beautiful
Cover photograph of Smokey Mountains in Gatlinburg, Tennessee, courtesy
of Doris Clayton. Type and design by Karen Stone.
Copyright ©2008 Bill McLaughlin. All rights reserved.
Published by Waldenhouse Publishers, Inc.
100 Clegg Street, Signal Mountain, TN 37377 USA
www.waldenhouse.com   888-222-8228
Printed in the United States of America
ISBN: 978-0-9814996-7-3
Library of Congress Control Number: 2008931107

Introduction

The situations and experiences related in the book are true. The stories told are shared that others, particularly my own children, may sense how life has changed in what appears to be a short period of time, and how God will come into our lives when we ask Him.

Beyond the Mountain is the story of a boy's life – a boy who was born into near poverty. Through continued faith, help from others and an internal desire to rise above the environment in which he found himself, he was able to obtain an education and achieve success in life.

During the thirties and forties, life in rural America was difficult. Factories were not yet established in the small towns of the South and expansion of the economy was not a term that was used openly. Families became transient only to find that life was hard regardless of their venue. Many adults, including some of my own brothers and sisters, made their way to larger northern cities such as Chicago, IL, Lansing MI, and South Bend, IN to find work and a better life style. Life in those days was like a mountain, difficult to reach the top.

There were many slips in my climb and the bluffs that confronted me were steep. Each challenge was approached one at a time. Some appeared insurmountable. My guide was always present leading the way. Upon reflection, which I have done many times, there is no explanation except to give Him credit for the path I took. There was no other way.

My hope is that all that choose to turn the pages of this book may lift something out that will be beneficial to them during their lifetime. More than this, my prayer is that they will find a deeper faith in God, a faith sufficient to provide the courage to climb their mountain and see the valley beyond.

Foreword

Only by written form can knowledge and events of time and of one's life be passed on for those who follow to remember. This book is provided that others, particularly my children and grandchildren, may get a glimpse of life in the first half of the 20th century in rural America.

More importantly, I hope they may learn how someone, even in those days, with the desire to learn and achieve could rise above near poverty, achieve a college degree and become a senior executive with a multi-billion dollar corporation. This book is the story of a sharecropper's son and the trials and tribulations experienced in his desire to climb above the economic level of those about him. The book contains real events, and it demonstrates how God opens doors when the key is lost. There may be someone out there struggling who has a dream. Hopefully this book will help that someone climb their mountain and realize their dream. It has happened before. It can happen again. Keep climbing.

"I'd like to add one thought to the subject of success and the claims made for it as a deserved reward for effort and understanding. It seems to me shallow and arrogant for any man in these times to claim he is completely self-made, that he owes all his success to his own unaided efforts. While, of course, it is basic Americanism that a man's standing is in part due to his personal enterprise and capacity, it is equally true that many hands and hearts and minds generally contribute to anyone's fate. We help create those circumstances which favor or challenge us in meeting our objectives and realizing our dreams. There is great comfort and inspiration in this feeling of close human relationships and its bearing on our mutual fortunes—a powerful force to overcome in the 'tough breaks' which are certain to come to most of us from time to time."   *Walter E. Disney (1901-1966)*

It Wasn't Done Alone

My life has been a miracle from my vantage point. Having said this, it needs to be stated that it was not done alone. How then can one express gratitude to all those who have contributed. Words are not sufficient but these are lifted up.

God. With Him all things are possible. He plotted my course.

My parents, poor and humble as they were, provided direction.

Brothers and sisters believed in me and gave me support.

Raymond Hale, Jr. saw something in me that made him want to help.

Mr. and Mrs. Raymond Hale, Sr. shared their home and provided assistance.

Mr. James Peery recognized a need and provided free meals at school.

Mrs. Mary Perry was a great lady who shared her home with many boys who needed help.

My wife Martha. Her love and devotion are constant.

My children, who are and have been my inspiration.

To all others, your prayers and support have helped immensely.

Contents

The Early Years 11

Bruceville 19

My Recollection 27

The War Years 31

Bruceville Becomes Home 37

Changing Times 51

How It All Began 65

Leaving Home 73

My Greates Challenge 79

A Plateau Was Reached 91

The Summit 97

The Valley Lies Ahead 111

We can make our plans;
but the Lord
determines our steps.

Proverbs 16:9

Chapter One
The Early Years

The fall of 1929 brought economic conditions never witnessed in the United States prior to that time. Soon thereafter the impact would be felt worldwide. The downturn was so devastating that it became known as the Great Depression. The conditions resulting from the collapse in the economy and financial institutions continued for approximately ten years for most of the country before any improvement could be witnessed. In many areas, particularly the rural sections, the depression would continue much longer. This was the longest and most severe of any recorded economic downturn in the U. S. and the world.

The U. S. economy was already suffering from a creditor position resulting from World War I. Post war debt had weakened the economy, contributing to the depression. With the catastrophic collapse of the New York Stock Exchange in October, 1929, the world was doomed economically. The downward spiral would continue for more than three years, and within this period the market had dropped more than 80 percent of its value prior to the collapse.

Everyone who had been fortunate enough to have savings accounts and other assets saw them eliminated before any action could be taken. Pressure was placed on all banks and financial institutions, and that compounded the problem. Banks that were caught with large portfolios, particularly stocks, saw their balance sheets change drastically. As a result, many of the financial institutions were forced into bankruptcy. By mid 1930, more than 1100 banks had failed, representing approximately 45 percent of banks at that time.

As a result of the other countries' dependency on the United States, the depression quickly spread to Europe and Asia and would eventually become worldwide. Like the U. S., many other countries, including Germany, were feeling the affects of the war and a weakness in their economies prior to 1929. Once the economic and financial crisis hit the U. S., and credit was shut off to European countries, prosperity collapsed.

The general consensus was that the economic conditions the country found itself in were as a result of the Republican president, Herbert Hoover. Today if one would mention President Hoover, the depression would be associated. Likewise if the Great Depression is part of conversation, the minds of those that experienced it would think of Hoover.

With the population feeling that a change had to be made, Franklin D. Roosevelt, a Democrat, was elected President in 1932. This was near the low point of the depression for most of the country. Roosevelt soon, through government regulations and programs, put into place public work programs that would assist the lower class to become employed. These programs would provide income for food to a starving population. While these programs helped immensely, approximately 15 percent of the workforce continued to be unemployed at the outbreak of World War II in 1939.

Much more could be said about the entire economy in those years. Stories were told of soup lines where people, for the first time in American history, were near starvation across the country. Stealing of food from the back of delivery trucks became so prevalent that guards had to be called in to protect the food. It was commonplace to eat black-eyed peas and cornbread or any other food for breakfast to obtain essential nourishment. Never before or since have the American people experienced conditions as found during the depression. Never have they suffered so much.

As previously mentioned, toward the end of the Great Depression work programs such as WPA and CCC, initiated by President Roosevelt, provided some relief to many people. Dams were constructed along the Tennessee River to harness water for the generation of electricity in north Alabama and in Tennessee. This provided a source of income to many of the laboring class of people, including my father. He would walk several miles to catch a work truck, ride to a distant work site, work all day and repeat the trip back home. He was part of the labor force that would build the Wilson and Joe Wheeler Dams in northern Alabama. It was later that the Pickwick Dam in Tennessee was constructed. The dams would prove to be the beginning of progress for rural America. Not only did the construction of the dams provide labor at a desperately needed time, but they also provided a source for generating electricity. Electricity would eventually replace coal and wood as fuel to heat homes and replace kerosene (coal oil) lamps for illumination of the homes.

This was the economic environment I was born into. The economic conditions were beginning to improve. However the laboring class was not the beneficiary of the early changes. Born on November 1, 1936, I would be the tenth child born to my parents, James Oscar and Pokie Inez McLaughlin. Unfortunately the first child had died of a disease called colitis that was common at that time.

It was not unusual for families to have large numbers of children. Agriculture was the largest employer in the rural South, and the thought was that a large family would be more productive in the fields. No consideration was given to the expenses of rearing the family, as they would eat from the gardens and animals raised on the farm. Clothes and shoes for winter (children usually went barefoot in summer) could be purchased or hand made. Education was of little concern for rural America.

Killen, Alabama, my birthplace, is a small community northeast of Florence. It was a common practice in those days for doctors to make house calls and for births to take place in the home as opposed to hospitals. The doctor would be alerted when the time was near, and he would come and remain until the baby's arrival. The house in which I was born contained four rooms and had wood siding and a tin roof. As was the standard in that time, the house had a flue for the exhaust of the fumes created by the wood stove. In those days wood was often used to fuel both the heating and cooking stoves. Electricity was an unknown commodity in rural America in the 1930's.

Neither Mom nor Dad were permitted an education. Being of rural parents themselves, an education was not easily attainable. Dad was from a family of nine children, and his dad had died when he was a teenager. He would say that he finished the second reader. When Mamma was eight, she was forced to help at home with her younger sister when her mother died.

The earning level of the family was low, and like most families, was dependent on some form of agriculture. Without an education there was little opportunity, outside of farming, for earning a living. Until the advent of electric power, developed through the construction of dams, the northern part of the state of Alabama with its red clay soil was not conducive to farming, and one can imagine what the economic conditions might have been.

The house where I was born. Killen, Alabama (Picture taken years later)

Give all your worries to Him
because He cares about you.

1 Peter 5:7

Chapter Two
Bruceville

Bruceville is a community located in Dyer County of western Tennessee. The western part of the county lies in the Mississippi River bottom and the eastern half is on a gently undulating ridge. Dyer County was settled by adventurous families moving from middle Tennessee to the west in search of a better livelihood. Bruceville was, and continues to be, very rural, and its people, for the most part, have minimal education. There is no written history known of the community. Accordingly, no one knows how it got its name, or why or how long ago it appeared as a trading center. The first mill in the county, for grinding corn and grain, was water-powered and built on Mill Creek which is about four miles from Bruceville. Given that much of the county was first developed in the general area, the community was most likely a trading location.

The names of Rutherford, Davidson, Hassels, Turpins and Weakleys arrived in Bruceville on horseback in the 1820's and 1830's. When they arrived the country was lush and the air fresh. The territory that had provided Native American Indians a prolific life of hunting, fishing and birthing of their families was encroached upon by the new inhabitants. Those that followed the early settlers found good soil for crop production, abundant timber of all varieties for home building, and wild life and fish for food. No doubt it appeared as a paradise.

The map on the following page provides the location of Dyer County and Bruceville. The community continues to be call Bruceville today, and the area stretches from old U. S. Highway 51 on the west side to almost Crockett County on the east side. The area encompasses several thousand acres of farmland held hostage during parts of the year by flooding of Pond Creek and Forked Deer River. Changes in farming techniques have impacted the community. Once populated with several hundred people, all friends and relatives, it is a quite peaceful community. The community includes churches of two protestant denominations, Baptist and Methodist. Many of the old family names are gone and have been replaced with new families.

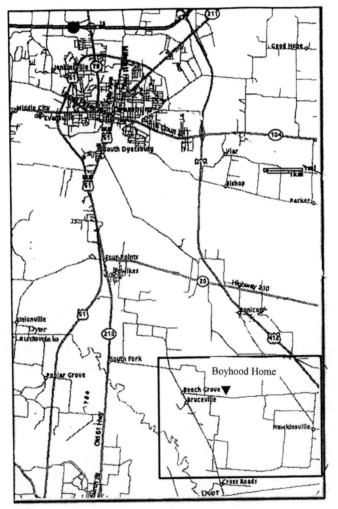

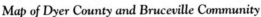

Map of Dyer County and Bruceville Community

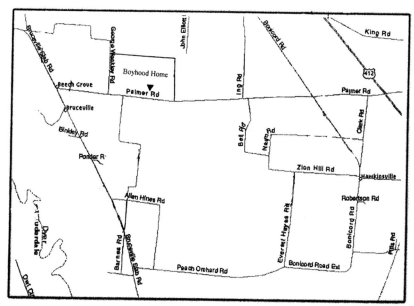

Bruceville Community

    During the 1930's several families of northern Alabama and Mississippi migrated to west Tennessee in search of more opportunity. Many of the families settled in the rural community known as Bruceville. Some of these families were friends and distant relatives of my Mom and Dad. The families included the Phillips, Williams, Stutts, Canadas and Hines. Receiving word bacl in Alabama that the Tennessee farmland was more productive than northern Alabama and the fact that work was plentiful, my parents decided to make the move in the fall of 1937. By this time some of my brothers and sisters were in their teens and could work in the fields to supplement the family income.

    At the time of the move, my first birthday had not arrived. The story is told that the family of nine children and all their "belongings" moved from Alabama to Tennessee in a three-quarter ton truck to work with Willie Lee Stutts, a cousin of my mother. The next year we moved into a house with a loft area, and it was in this house that the shadows of "Recollection" begin to occur.

After living there only a few months, we moved again to the Weakley Farm where many day laborers living in the community worked. It was in this community that lifelong childhood friends were made and roots established that continue today.

Murray Hudson, a descendant of one of the pioneering families to settle the community and an educator, stockbroker-turned-farmer with his father, authored a book titled *Dirt and Duty* which had the community of Bruceville as its setting. The following paragraphs as well as other descriptions of the community are taken from Mr. Hudson's book, with his permission, to give some flavor to the citizenry of that community.

"FOLK KNOWLEDGE

"My Bruceville neighbors stake out a pretty wide field of basic knowledge. Prather can see a water dog (a smudge of rainbow colors) in the nearly clear sky and predict rain in two days, even in a drought. And every cold spell in late spring has a name: blackberry winter, locust winter, and dogwood winter…

"Because people like Moody Palmer have lived seventy springs in close companionship with the out-of-doors, they felt those chill days when the honey locust bloomed with dangling white clusters like grapes. It happened again and again, and they named it and remembered.

"They are equally acquainted with the earth they walk on, plant in, and will be planted in someday. They prefer rich, deep black 'barn yard' dirt for gardens. Slick red clay that holds moisture in a drought but bakes out like brick (and is used for bricks) they plant in okra, or its cousin cotton. Sticky gray 'gumbo' clay in the bottoms (so richly scented it recalls old outhouse digging) produces great soybeans. They call the white ground on Pond Creek side of the ridge 'buckshot.' It is crumbly, poor and full of hard nodules and barely holds the earth together.

"Miss Bessie Haley knows to plant 'taters' and other root vegetables in the dark of the moon. She plants above ground vegetables by the half or full moon. And anything planted on Good Friday thrives.

"Folk hereabouts predict severity of coming winter several ways. A cracked persimmon seed has either a 'fork' or a 'spoon' to show the harshness. Wooly worms or caterpillars with wide stripes augur for a cold winter, and you can tell how deep the snow will be by the lowest wasp nest.

"All these sayings come from acute observation of the natural world by people who have had to deal with it day in and day out for generations."

There were many prevalent "sayings" in the country life. Many words were coined and accepted only among the country folk. Only true southerners who lived and worked together during these times could understand this rural language. Such expressions as a "hissie fit" and "conniption" might describe an unhappy child, but you had to know that you don't "have" them you "pitch" them. No one but country people could tell you how many turnip greens or butter beans it took to make a "mess."

If you needed directions you had to understand the general direction of "yonder." And a "good piece" could mean a mile or five miles. All country folk grew up knowing that "directly" meant that you would return in a little while. No one knew what a noun, verb or adverb meant, but they did know that you could use the word "fixin" any way you wanted to. The true southern country people knew that "dinner" was the big meal of the day and was served at noon along with sweet tea that tasted better out of a "fruit jar." What is "left over" is supper to be enjoyed again as the evening meal. You didn't lock the door, you "buttoned" the door. If you heard someone say, "Well I called myself looking," you knew you were in the presence of a real southerner. If you could not accept these and similar expression, you could not qualify as a southerner.

A "day laborer" was a person who worked on someone else's farm and was paid by the hour or day for their labor. Such a person or family was provided a house to live in and generally work of some type. Work could include anything from planting, plowing or harvesting of the crops to hay bailing and mending of fences or clearing the fence rows. However day laborers owned no property or equipment of any type. They had their own freedom and could move about wherever they chose. Other than that, they were servants to the landlord. They were totally dependent on the landlord for all their needs. If a doctor was needed, the landlord paid the expense and deducted the charges from wages the next week. In many places, the landlord even owned the store that supplied the food and clothing. These day laborers lived from day to day with little hope of improving their lifestyle. The landowner extracted everything except an existence.

During this period of time gas powered farm equipment was not yet developed to the extent that it was used on most farms. Equipment used in the farming operation was quite crude in comparison to today's standards, and the power for the essential equipment was mules. Today a mule is a rare commodity, and to see one is unusual.

In 1939 my Dad decided to venture out and become a "Sharecropper." We moved to what the family referred to as the Inman Place. This was in the Bonicord community, some three miles from Bruceville. A sharecropper was usually a family unit who would live on property owned by some landlord. The landlord would provide the land, equipment, mules, feed and the other expenses of the farm. The family would farm the land and give the landlord a percentage of the yield, usually fifty percent. This would be considered a step up from the classification of day laborers. While better than a day laborer, a sharecropper was looked down upon, and the word itself denoted a lower economic class of people.

It was the sharecroppers that fed the nation in those years. Economically they were deprived, and like people today without an education, to move out of this environment was difficult, in fact almost impossible. However more importantly, while economically deprived, they were rich in spirit and family values. Right and wrong were taught in the home, and many a tree limb has been broken and cotton stalk pulled out of the ground to provide attitude adjustments as necessary. These years nourished my roots and a built a foundation to guide and sustain me into the future.

He who began
a good work in you
will carry it on to completion…

Philippians 1:6

Chapter Three
My Recollection

Recollection is a term often used by my dad during his lifetime. It is seldom heard today, but would relate to one's memory. How appropriate for this chapter to commence with these words.

My recollection of life begins when I was approximately two years of age, but only a shadow or two remain. A more vivid memory commenced as a three-year-old. Such things as being flogged by a neighbor's rooster and the stile that crossed the fence on our frequented path are most vivid. The events prior to my recall are important as they outline life for the lower working class of peoples in the first half of the twentieth century.

Sometime between the harvesting of the crops and the planning for another year, sharecroppers would bargain for the next year. They would either reach agreement with the current landlord to remain where they were or bargain with another landowner to move onto his farm. We did this a lot. As a matter of fact, we moved six times the first six years of my life.

We lived on the Inman Farm only one year, as my dad entered into an agreement with J. Z. Espy to move onto his farm back into the Bruceville community. Unlike today all the agreements reached between the landlord and tenant farmer were oral agreements. Seldom was anything reduced to writing. Obviously, verbal agreements permitted misunderstandings and disagreements to occur which often happened for one reason or another.

Mr. and Mrs. Espy had three children: Sue, Royce and Geraldine. Royce was my age and we had many childhood disagreements but became great friends as we grew older. Their parents are now deceased, but the children continue to reside in the Bruceville community today.

By 1940 my two older sisters had married, leaving seven children and my parents as the family at home. The Espy farmhouse we lived in only had three rooms: a living room, bedroom and kitchen. Usually the living room would double as a bedroom due to the need for sleeping space. Our mattresses on the beds were made of straw removed from the fields and enclosed by hand made cotton covers. There were no pesticides in those days, and it was not uncommon to look under the bed and find chinch bugs everywhere. The larva of the bugs had been laid in the field and was hatched after the straw had been brought inside. There was no easy way to dispense of these critters. We lived there one year and then moved near the Friendship community into a larger home and onto the farm owned by Lowell Hawkins.

The Hawkinses had a son whose name was DeWayne, and we became life-long friends. Strange as it may be, DeWayne and I live in Germantown, Tennessee, today and see each other two or three times a year. My family lived in that community two years and much happened in those years. It was here that I started to school, a three-room building with two teachers who taught eight grades. Unlike today, only the three "R's" – reading, riting and rithmetic – were taught. The third room was used as a school cafeteria, and mothers would pair up and cook the meals for the children. They received no compensation for their labor, however they were able to be sure the children had a balanced meal as the county and state provided the food. The school had no electricity, and heat was provided in the wintertime by coal burning stoves. It is interesting that the name of the school was Dyer College.

One memory I have of this time is a trip a to Friendship with two of my brothers. Friendship was approximately four miles from where we lived. My brothers were sent to Jack Carmen's store, where we traded (shopped) at that time for staples, to pick up a needed item, and I went along. While at the store I found a small package of crackers and proceeded to take them with me. Realizing that this was not the thing to do, I kept them out of sight of everyone until we returned home and then proceeded to open the package. My mother, realizing that the crackers were taken without payment, required one of my brothers and me to return the crackers and apologize for taking them. It was a lesson learned that has not been forgotten.

The old log barn that the neighborhood kids and my brothers played in, and the fun they had playing such games a corncob jail, hide and seek, and other games will never be forgotten. Getting into the nearby stock pond was another fun thing to do, even though it was most unhealthy.

All who listen to me
will live in peace and safety,
unafraid of harm.

Proverbs 1:33

Chapter Four
The War Years

The bombing of Pearl Harbor by the Japanese on December 7, 1941, occurred while we were living in the Friendship community. The surprise attack by the Japanese brought the United States into the war. This was a troublesome time for the entire world, particularly those families in the United States who had sons in their late teens. It was a requirement in those years that all young men present themselves by registration for the military draft at the age of 18. In 1942 my oldest brother was called into service, as were most young men. I can easily remember the sadness that permeated throughout our household. Fortunately he never had to serve in battle. The war changed the lives of many people, including my family.

I have fond memories of these years. We walked to school in those days, and there was always something happening on the way or on our return home – things like my brothers getting into an apple orchard owned by neighbors, robbing the pecan trees in the fall or getting into a disagreement with someone in the group. As we moved down the road toward the school, other children would join in the walk, and by the time we arrived there was a large group. A large ditch near where we lived had a lot of sand and a spring, the type where water would push itself to the surface. The spring was underground exposing itself to the bank of the ditch and provided cool water considered suitable for drinking. It was an excellent place to play.

By 1943 World War II was being fought on many fronts. Europe, Africa and the South Pacific were being bombarded

inland as well as well as on the waterfronts. There was a new fo-
cus, a new attitude among all American people. Never before and
certainly not since, have the American people come together to
support a cause like that experienced during this period of time.
Servicemen were looked upon and treated as heroes whether or
not they had been involved in battle. Anyone in uniform was
given great respect.

In early 1943, we moved to yet another community with the
name of Cross Roads. All these communities were four or five
miles apart. Our year at this location was somewhat uneventful.
We lived down a long lane that became almost beyond travel
in the winter months. This did not present any great problem
however, since we did not have a car. As a matter of information,
when we needed shoes or clothes we traveled to Halls, the nearest town, in a wagon drawn by mules. Here I met and became
great friends with Wayne Wyrick, who would be another friend
for life, and his parents Paul and Ruth. Miss Ruth, as she was
referred to, would later tell me she tried to adopt me, but my
parents would not let her.

Only a few years ago, I received a telephone call from Wayne,
and he asked me if I would consider being a pallbearer at his dad's
funeral. He indicated that his mother wanted him to ask me, and
that his dad would have wanted it also. A little math would relate
that some 50 plus years had passed since our meeting. I appreciated the invitation and served with sadness.

By 1944 the war had escalated and many countries were now
involved. It truly was a world war. We had moved to Rob Taylor's
place, a farm that had been purchased by J. Z. Espy that same
year. This was the same landowner on whose farm we had lived
in 1941. The location of this farm was between the Bruceville
and Cross Roads Communities. We were the first family to oc-
cupy the house after Mr. Taylor, the previous owner, had vacated.

It was the best house we had lived in. However, it too was down a long dirt lane that was impassible by vehicle during the winter months. There were two other houses farther down the lane beyond our house. Otherwise the road led nowhere except to the Old River and where the river widened into Fitzhugh Eddy.

Fitzhugh Eddie was a spot for much enjoyment during the summer. It was a swimming hole, a fishing spot, and a picnic area. Some families would travel to the spot by wagon or trailer pulled by mules, take food, drink and chairs and spend the Fourth of July enjoying the water, woods and nature. It was a place where baptismal services were often performed. Like Jesus, many people were baptized in the river in those days. Today there are no houses down the lane and the lane itself has been included with the farmland on either side.

While we were living in this house we received our first electricity to provide lighting. All our previous houses had been illuminated with kerosene lamps that provided very little candle-power. Only those who experienced living with these lamps can be appreciative of electricity. The kerosene lamps were a little better than candles, but not much.

Most metals were being used in the production of military vehicles and equipment, so there were no electrical appliances being manufactured for home use. Metals were scarce, and a lead penny was minted in 1943 since copper was in so much demand for military production. This was the only such coin ever minted. Even if metals had been available, our family was much too poor to have purchased appliances.

Several types of foods and condiments were rationed, including black pepper, sugar and coffee, and stamps were required to purchase gas. All these items were reserved for the military, and food stamps were issued and rationed for families to have some of these commodities. We ate almost no meat during this period

Gasoline Ration Card

Mileage ration card

The United States government issued ration cards and books during World War II.

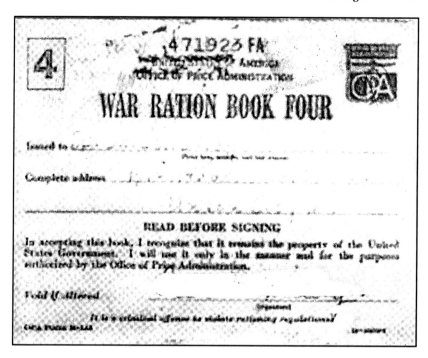

due to its scarcity and the fact that no money was available. Farm animals were not even being raised for slaughter during this time. One of my most vivid memories of this time was our dining table made of poplar planks and two benches extending the length of the table made from rough sawn wood. Mom and Dad had a chair at either end of the table, and the six children remaining at home would line up at the sides on the benches.

By this time there were a few cars moving up and down the bumpy country roads. In order to start the cars it was necessary to use a crank on the outside of the car, as there were no keyed switches or starters. The crank turned the crankshaft that would in turn move the cylinders and ignite the spark to the gas. If one was not careful the car would start, and the crank would remain engaged, causing it to whirl around striking one's hand or arm.

The war ended with the signing of the truce on November 11, 1945, that later came to be known as Armistice Day. A holiday is given now for this historical event, and we now refer to it as Veterans Day.

The McLaughlin children, from left: Bill, Emma Jean, Charles, Onzie, B.W., Bess, James, Marie and Mae. Picture taken in 1945. Notice access lane to house.

Dad with a team of Mules, Kit and Tige (1945)

Give your worries to the Lord,
and He will take care of you.
He will never let you down

Psalm 55:22

Chapter Five
Bruceville
Becomes Home

In 1946 we moved back to the community of Bruceville, some three miles away, on a farm that was being rented by my brother-in-law. A farmer who rented land was considered above a sharecropper, as he had his own equipment and mules. However,

Dad and Horace, my brother-in-law, preparing a two row planter for planting cotton (1947)

a renter usually paid most of the expenses of the farm. Usually the landowner would contribute some toward seed or fertilizer and, of course, provide the land. A renter would get from two-thirds to three-fourths of the crop yield, and the landowner would get the balance. This move would prove to be thought of as the home place, since we lived here the balance of my childhood.

Dad and Donnie, my nephew, on the planter (1947)

I was nine years old when we moved onto this farm and my parents lived there until my junior year in high school. This is where many of my childhood memories were created. The farm-houses were not built on foundations but elevated off the ground by Poplar Tree blocks with open crawl spaces underneath. Many hours were spent underneath the house playing in the dirt. It was always a cool dry spot to play in the summertime. However, the house had no underpinning or insulation, and the cold of the winter would make its way under the house. If there was a crack in the floors that was not covered, you could see light through the floors as well as through the walls.

We had a Beech Tree in the front yard and the bark of this tree was receptive to carving of initials and short messages. All the boys in the community, and some adults, would come and visit and carve their initials and those of their favorite girl friends. The tree remains until this day, as do the initials of all who came by.

Pond Creek ran nearby this farm, and it was the spot for fishing, for boys skinny-dipping in the summer time, for shooting BB guns at turtles and frogs, and for generally just killing time. My BB gun was acquired from selling garden and flower seeds that were obtained from a company in Lancaster, Pennsylvania. When a certain amount of seeds were sold, a prize could be chosen. The BB gun was my choice as there was no money available to buy one. A friend of mine, Caron Rice, and I spent a lot of time in the Pond Creek area and had great fun at the creek with our guns. Unlike today, when children have more toys than they can play with, we had almost no purchased toys except for possibly a top, yo-yo or sponge ball. We found it convenient to make our toys. Thing like "Tom Walkers" made from two tin cans turned upside down with holes in the sides where hay bailing wire could be threaded through and extended so the wire could be grasped with the hands, or a "Scotch Wheel," a metal ring from the broken hub of a wagon with a home made paddle to push it with, were common toys for boys.

There was a family who lived on the east side of the creek with the name of Woods. The family consisted of Frank, his wife and their son, John Ed. If anyone in the community was poorer, less educated and un-bathed than we, it was this family. No one

Beech Tree (Picture taken in 1994)

Close-up of Beech Tree (Notice Initials Remaining)

knew the ages of Frank or John Ed, but it would have appeared that John Ed was probably born soon after Frank and his wife were married. Frank and John Ed seldom bathed or shaved, both chewed tobacco and were almost illiterate. Everyone in the community knew them. The story goes that one day when Frank and John Ed were at the country store, one of the men in the community asked John Ed who was older, he or his father. After some time and consideration, John Ed replied that he thought "Paw was a lilliest older." The family was so recognized in the community for their habits that one of my brothers acquired the nickname of John Ed, and my brother-in-law was called Frank. They carried these nicknames until their deaths.

Bruceville was positioned to receive much of the weather from the northwest and particularly weather with tornadic conditions. Several homes were damaged and destroyed through the years as these storms would move eastward through the community. My parents were afraid of the storms that frequented the area in the spring of the year. Dad would build a storm house out of railroad ties, and we would spend parts of many spring nights in the storm house. Often he would get us out of bed, rush to the storm house, wait there until the storm passed and go back inside the house and return to bed. It wasn't unusual for this to happen two or three times in one night.

In the smoke house was kept the meat that was cured in winter, the lard that was rendered from the cuttings from the hogs when slaughtered, and other staples that were preserved from the garden and canned in jars.

Most of the year's supply of pork was killed and preserved. Usually in the late fall or early winter months after the weather had stabilized at cooler temperatures it would be nearing the time to kill hogs. However, this could not be done just any day. The old timers would watch the weather patterns, and once the temperature was near freezing and no sudden changes in the weather conditions were apparent for several days, they would kill hogs. They did not have a television or newspaper to give them a seven-day forecast to go by.

Often several neighbors or friends would come together for this event. Early in the morning of the day planned for the slaughter, a fire would be built under a large vat that was used for scalding the hogs. The hogs would usually be shot with a rifle and the throats immediately cut so that the blood could drain. This was necessary for preservation of the meat. The hog would then be transferred directly to the vat and rolled in the hot water permitting removal of the hair.

Once this was accomplished, the animal was placed in a vertical position held by its back legs on a rack previously constructed. This would permit the dressing of the hog and further draining of liquids from the animal. Late in the day one of the more experienced men would block out the hog. This essentially would be cutting the hog into large pieces such as the shoulders, hams, sides, etc. These would be laid out in the smoke house overnight to permit the heat inside the animal to escape.

Usually the next day or the second day, the parts would be trimmed in preparation of the curing process. Edible organs such as the liver would be saved. The heads and less desirable parts would receive special attention and were usually used to make a special pressed meat called souse. When all the heat had escaped from the animals, the meat would be rubbed in a special salt and placed in a large wood container and then covered with the salt. This was the curing process. When left for approximately six weeks the meat was then removed and the pieces with bones and joints (hams and shoulders) would be covered in large meat sacks to prevent flies from spoiling the meat when warm weather came. The fat would be cut away from the choice cuts and would be cooked to separate or render the liquid fat from the meat. This liquid, when cooled, would harden and become lard or a form of cooking oil. As can be seen, little was wasted.

We had a large vegetable garden each year together with truck patches where food for the winter would be grown and preserved. Truck patches were larger areas of ground devoted to a particular vegetable such as peas, beans, corn, etc. Much of the summer time was used to preserve the food. Vegetables were preserved by canning in glass jars commonly know as fruit jars. Lima beans and peas were often permitted to dry in the hull and would be shelled and kept in containers to keep weevils out. Sometimes fruit would be peeled, sliced and dried in the sun as a form of preservation for later use. Everything possible was done to eliminate the need to purchase food.

Dad Making Ready The Garden With a One-Mule Breaking Plow (1948)

We had a cow that provided the milk for the family. Late in the afternoon we would herd the cow from the pasture to the barnyard for milking. All the kids learned to milk at an early age, as this was an essential chore.

Wood could be obtained from nearby, and it would be cut to proper lengths by a cross cut saw and split to be used for heating and cooking during the winter. This was a chore for my Dad and older brothers. However, I did have plenty of opportunity to sit on the rack, holding the wood down as it was being cut. It was also part of my chores to bring in the wood for use by the stoves.

Electricity was available at this time. However we did not have any electrical appliances. Even the radio was operated from a battery. The cost of the electricity prohibited its use for heating and cooling, as was the cost of the units to provide such accommodations. Since we had no refrigeration we used the service of an iceman who would travel through the country, usually twice a week in the summer. We had a piece of cardboard with 25, 50, 75 and 100 on each side of it. The procedure was to place the card in the window with the amount of ice you wanted at the top. We would purchase a block of ice usually weighing 100 pounds. The ice was protected from melting so quickly by wrapping it up with quilts and paper and placing it under a galvanized wash tub.

An interesting side note is the fact that my dad would go to the woods and cut a small hickory sapling (tree) and have it pulled home by a mule or hauled in a wagon. He would then, by use of a special knife, carve small strips of the bark from the sapling and use it to place a bottom (seat) in our chairs. The hickory bottoms would last forever. As a matter of documentation, a chair that my dad placed a bottom in sits in our house today as a reminder of the period. It is estimated that the bottom in that chair has been there more than fifty years, and it will probably last another fifty years if the chair is not discarded.

All water used for drinking, cooking, cleaning and bathing was drawn from a well in the front yard. The drawing of the water was accomplished by lowering a long cylindrical bucket down into the ground, letting it fill with water and then pulling it back up, emptying it into the water bucket, and carrying it inside to be used. The entire family, plus any visitors, drank out of the same dipper that was returned to the bucket when one was finished. All bathing came either from a wash pan or tub with the water being obtained as described. Any warm or hot water either had to be placed outside in the sun or on the stove in a cast iron kettle to

Mom with the well in the background. Notice the bucket at the well and the wash tub at right. (1949)

heat. It was not until later years that the more formal galvanized kettles were introduced.

Christmas has always been celebrated as the birth of Christ.

This was no exception in rural America in the thirties and forties. However, our celebration did not start with shopping at Thanksgiving to get prepared for December 25th. As one might gather, no shopping malls existed in those days, and there were very limited funds available for gifts. Usually the married adults of the family would present gifts of limited value to Mom and Dad. However, Mom and Dad did not have the ability to provide gifts in return. The children at home would usually be presented with a gift of some type, but usually very inexpensive. Our Christmas morning would more likely be a display of fruits and nuts laid out someplace within the room.

Our celebration of Christmas usually would commence with baking activities the week before Christmas Day and the boiling of a country ham that had been cured. All the family would gather on Christmas day for a large meal. It would not be unusual for there to be three or four different types of cakes and an equal number of pies baked. Usually we would then extend the celebration by going to one of the older brother's or sister's homes for a similar meal for the next couple of days.

One of the most interesting parts of country life was watching the animals. All of them have peculiar habits. When the harness was taken off the mules they would lie down and turn themselves in the grass as if to roll over. It was a common saying that if the mule could roll all the way over he was worth a million dollars. Another fun thing was watching as the hen would lead her brood of little chickens around the yard and help them find food. Sometimes in inclement weather or if danger presented itself, the mother hen would gather her chicks under her wings by a carefully executed sweeping motion. Perhaps the most amazing of all was watching the chickens move toward the chicken house at the end of the day and establish their position on the roosting poles for the night. The crowing of the roosters to signal the start a new day was always a part of the daybreak.

Through the years the term "Nest Egg" has remained. Today these words are used in connection with money or in a financial manner. The genesis of the words is directly from the country. When a hen was laying eggs it was important that at least one egg remained in the nest if more eggs were to be expected. Otherwise, the hen would simply move her nest to some place more difficult to find so the eggs could not be taken.

Humble yourself
before the Lord
and He will pick you up.

James 4:10

Chapter Six.
Changing Times

The war was over and people were beginning to settle into a new lifestyle. All the energies and attention that were contributed to the war were now directed to other things. Cars were being manufactured again. Electricity was being extended throughout rural America, and home appliances were becoming more plentiful but not affordable to everyone.

Our immediate family continued to reduce as brothers and sisters married and formed new households. By 1948 only four children remained at home. My dad continued to sharecrop with my brother-in-law.

Earlier in their lives my parents had lived near a Church of Christ and had joined that denomination. However there were no churches of this denomination around the country where we lived, so all my brothers, sisters and I attended the Baptist Church in Bruceville. I remember the night in a revival when I joined the church and also remember hitching a ride to a church in Dyersburg to be baptized. Mother and Dad did not have transportation and did not attend my baptismal service.

One of my fondest memories of life in the country was Sunday. There is an expression around today associated with dinner that is "Like Sunday On The Farm." Sunday was a big day at our house. My brothers and sisters would bring their families and come visit all day. Often we had uninvited friends who would stop by and stay for lunch (dinner as it was called in the country) with us. My mother never knew on Sunday morning whom she would be cooking for at noon. Often there would be so many people we would have three sittings. Usually the adult males would eat first, then the children and then the ladies. Said differently the table would be large enough for only one third of the people to eat at one time. The food would never be fancy, perhaps an occasional beef roast, or fried chicken that had been plucked from the yard that morning. You could always bet there would be plenty of whatever we were having.

The dishes would be washed in a large dishpan, as there were no utilities to supply water. After everyone had eaten, the food remaining would be placed at one end of the table and covered with a tablecloth to be uncovered and eaten at the next meal.

In the afternoon everyone sat out under the shade trees and visited for several hours. The children would involve themselves in such games as corn cob jail, hide and seek, and ball games, or they would roll their scotch wheels or just sit and listen to the experiences of the older family members.

There was little to do on the farm from the time the crops were harvested until spring. As spring arrived the cotton and corn stalks from the previous year were cut and the land was prepared for planting of the new crops. Most of the row crop in those days consisted only of cotton, corn and hay. Cotton was the money crop from which the farmers derived their living, and the corn and hay were reserved for the farm animals. Occasionally we would take some of the field corn to the mill and have it ground for chicken feed or to have it milled for bread.

Usually farming would commence as soon as the temperatures would get above freezing in the spring. This would generally be in late February or early March. By this time some of the more established farmers were beginning to buy small tractors and more sophisticated equipment. However, renters and sharecroppers continued with more traditional and crude methods of farming.

The cotton would usually be planted in April and the corn in May or June. All the ground was broken or turned by a mule drawn plow called a breaking plow. It was necessary to plow the soil as deeply as possible to turn the richer soil to the top and to loosen it for planting. Once the soil was broken, disked and harrowed to level it, another plow was used to bed the soil. Bedding was just a word used for establishing the rows for planting. Planting was done by a piece of equipment with hoppers to hold the seed. There were one-row and two row planters. It was necessary for the farmer to walk behind the one-row planter. However the two-row equipment had a seat where one could ride. Today very large equipment is used, and often some crops are planted without interrupting the soil. This is referred to as "no till" planting.

Left to right, front row: Charles, Billy, Onzie;
second row: James (Bo), Dad, and B.W.

Mom and Dad (1950)

The crops required a great deal of manual labor in those days. There were no chemicals to control the weeds and grasses as there are today. Pesticides were not used for boll weevils and other insects, and defoliants were non-existent. Cotton usually had to be chopped with hoes twice each year. Once to thin the cotton and clean what vegetation was crowding the plants and then a second time to eliminate new grasses and weeds that could not be controlled with the plows. Chopping the cotton required a person to physically walk each row from one end to the other with their eyes continually focused on the row so as not to over-look any unwanted vegetation. Care was taken not to damage the cotton with the hoe as the weeds and grass were removed. It was always a fight to keep ahead of the Johnson grass, cockleburs, morning glories and other forms of unwanted vegetation. Chemi-cals and more sophisticated equipment have now replaced the need for cotton chopping.

A pleasant memory of those days is the scene of a rain show-er moving across the field and the scent of the earth's soil that preceded the shower. You could literally smell the rain moving toward you.

Mule drawn cultivators with different types of plows were used to continue turning the soil to stimulate growth and remove unwanted vegetation. The work was hot and tiring, but there was no other way. Usually we were able to complete the cleaning of our crop and then would "hire out" our labor to other farmers in the community. This was a way of earning a little money. The pay was fifty cents per hour, and everyone usually worked ten-hour days. Before my sister and I were old enough to hire out for a full hand (employee), we would work together and receive the wages of one employee.

Air conditioning was non-existent in the country, and we used the breeze coming through the open windows and screen doors to provide cool air during the summer months. The exte-rior doors had no locks and were held closed by a wooden button turned cross wise. Security was not a problem in the country in those days.

The early evening, which was the usual bedtime, was gener-ally too warm to go to sleep immediately. Often we would lie in bed being entertained by the katydids, crickets and other outside insects sounding their mating calls. The outside filled with light-ning bugs created an electric frenzy. In the distance we could hear a frog bellowing its location in the stock pond to the opposite sex, or the whoo, whoo, whoo of an owl, or a steam engine ap-proaching the intersection of Bruceville Road with Highway 51. As the air moved gently through the open windows a scent of honeysuckle or the sweet smell of an over ripe strawberry patch could be detected. Eventually, the bodies tired from the days work would succumb to the heat and fall asleep.

There were no bath facilities in most of the homes in the country. After working in the fields all day we would usually wash our hands, faces, and feet and retire for the evening. No full bath was taken except on Saturdays. Usually washtubs would be filled with water drawn from the well in the morning and left out in the sun to warm it. The weekly bath was then taken at noon or whenever the workday ended.

Corn did not require so much attention as did the cotton. On occasion we would have to walk through the corn cutting out the larger pieces of vegetation and doing some thinning. How-ever it was much quicker than cotton chopping. Cutting, raking and bailing hay was never a pleasant chore. This was always done in late summer after the Jap or Alfalfa, a form of foliage grown for livestock, was matured. It was an extremely hot, uncomfortable job, as the chaff from the hay would tend to collect on a person's heated body and get inside your clothes. The job was left to the older males.

The hay would be cut with a mower and left to dry in the field to eliminate all moisture. This was done to prevent the hay from mildewing once it was put into bales. The bailer was set up out in the field, and hay was brought to it and fed into the hopper. A mule hitched to a long pole circled the bailer to provide power for the bales to be produced. The circling motion of the pole acted like a crank that turned the gears of the bailer. As the hay was fed into the hopper it was compacted by the turning of the gears. Blocks made out of wood would be stuffed into the bailer as separators. There would be a man on each side of the bailer who would push wire through the bailer at the blocks to tie the bales together before they were pushed out the end of the bailer. This process was repeated over and over until all the loose hay had been converted into bales. Once completed the hay was hauled to the barn and placed in the loft until it was needed to feed the animals. Cutting, bailing and storage of the hay were the most disliked farm chores.

During this period of the year there was absolutely no money available. All crops had been "laid by," a term used in the country when all cultivating had ended and crops were maturing for harvest. There were no opportunities for earning money. Everyone anxiously waited, as did the store merchants, until September when the cotton could be picked and transported to the gins where it was sold and money generated. Many of the merchants permitted the farmers to use credit facilities during the summer months and were glad to be repaid in the fall.

All cotton was gathered by hand in those days and placed in a pick sack that trailed each picker. Fall nights would be cool, and the dew in the mornings often appeared like rain. In the mornings we would arise early and walk to the far end of the field so that we could pick back toward the wagon. This eliminated having to carry a heavy sack of cotton a great distant to have it emptied. We would sometimes be wet from the dew absorbed by our clothes. The "pick sack," as it was called, was placed around the head and one shoulder and extended behind the picker. A sack could hold about 50 to 60 pounds when packed full. When most pickers would fill their pick sacks, everyone would go to the wagon to have their bags weighed and emptied. A good cotton picker could gather some 300 pounds in a single day and would generally be paid $2.50 to $3.00 per hundred pounds.

Cotton Pickers. Notice the Pick Sacks. Photo courtesy of Pat Higdon.

In the country we would go back to summer school after the cotton was chopped, and then school would be let out for six weeks in the fall to gather the cotton. This was a very tiring chore as each picker had to keep his back bent over to reach the cotton. Most children were involved in picking, and my dad was not an exception to the rule. We went to the fields before the dew was off the leaves in the morning and would stay there until we could hardly see in the evenings, stopping only to empty the sacks and take some time for lunch. The cotton usually had to be gone over twice, and then the scrap bolls would be pulled and sold at discounted market prices. Unfortunately, by this time the weather had turned cold; the ground would be frozen, and gathering these scraps was most unpleasant. Sometimes one's hands would get so cold that they would hurt. Notwithstanding the

Sheet taken from actual cotton picking record book. Notice that each weight was multiplied by 3 to indicate three cents earned for each poiund of cotton picked.

discomfort, these scraps often represented what money would be left over after all expenses of the year were paid.

Once the crops were harvested and sold, and all loans for the year were repaid, only enough money remained to buy essential clothing and staples such as flour, meal and sugar for the winter months. If we had an opportunity to hire out and pick cotton or pull bolls for another farmer, we would generally get to use this money toward extra clothes or perhaps have a little better Christmas.

Sometime in 1948 or 1949 we purchased an icebox. This was not a refrigerator cooled by electricity but a heavily insulated and lined wooden cabinet which would keep ice for an extended period of time and provide cooling for milk and keep other foods from spoiling. (My wife often questions me today when I refer to the refrigerator as an icebox. However after many years of no other means of refrigeration, the name is hard to dismiss.)

A hole had to be cut through the wood floor in the kitchen to permit the water from the melted ice to escape. Aquiring an icebox was a big step up for us. A few years later we were able to buy a real refrigerator that would freeze water into ice in trays and keep other foods preserved. One cannot imagine not having these amenities unless they have lived before they existed or were affordable.

There was usually one day each week set aside for wash day. The water would be heated outside in the wash pot, a large black iron kettle, and transferred into the washtubs. The fire would be built on the side of the pot in the direction of the wind so as to permit the fire to be blown under the pot as opposed to away from it. One tub would be used for washing the clothes and one for rinsing. The washing consisted of rubbing bar soap on the clothes and then rubbing them against the metal rub board. Often the soap had been made at home using grease from the animals when they were killed. The grease was mixed with a product called lye. This type of soap would be referred to as "lye soap." Once the dirt was removed from the clothes, at least to a point, the item would be wrung out by hand to eliminate all soap possible, and then the garments would be placed in the rinse water. There might be a separate tub for the white pieces. If so, "bluing," a blue liquid, powder or bar would be placed in the tub as a whitening element. There was no product like Purex or Clorox in those days. Once this process had been completed, the clothes would be hung outside on a clothesline or fence to dry.

The next appliance that we acquired was a washing machine. It was a wringer type and not a washer and dryer. However, it was a huge improvement over the rub board that had been used in the past. With this new appliance the clothes could be washed in the machine by the agitator and wrung partially dry by the wringers. This eliminated a tremendous amount of work for the housewife.

By 1949 my last two brothers and one sister had married and moved north to work in factories in Illinois, Indiana or Michigan. This is the path that many of the young families chose to get away from the hard country life and the farm.

One who never experienced life as it was in rural America during the thirties, forties and fifties cannot visualize or imagine the simple life style. It was hard; it was difficult, but love within and outside the family was abundant. My Mother thought nothing of sending my sister or me up the road to a neighbor's house to borrow a cup of whatever she needed at the time to cook with. Likewise, our neighbors often called upon us, borrowing whatever they needed. It was a community of love, and everyone appreciated the position and need of those about them. In joy or sorrow, neighbors were neighbors.

These stray thoughts of years past cling like the tufts of ungathered cotton on spent stalks. Thoughts of the whirlwind blowing up dust on a hot summer day signifying continued drought conditions. The smell of rain as it pitted the dust and blew across the field, bringing a welcomed breeze as it passed. The Monarch butterflies dancing in the sunlight on a hot summer day. The earth pulls like a magnet to one's life raised by the soil. Thus the expression "You can take the boy out of the country, but you can't take the country out of the boy."

In those days when someone died, they usually were brought back to the home for the interim period before burial. There were community cemeteries where the men of the community would gather to prepare the grave. I shall never forget a statement made by one of the men in the community. He said that when my Dad died he wanted to know about it so that he could assist in the preparation of his grave, because he could never remember a time when my Dad was not there to assist in the grave preparation of others.

Dad and Mom were some of the poorest in the community in terms of family assets, but they were rich in many ways. I would be elated if my "balance sheet" in life looked like theirs.

When all my brothers and sisters left home, it was probably the low point in my life. I was thirteen years old living with only Mom and Dad now. There was absolutely nothing to do for enjoyment in the evenings. TVs were not affordable to most rural people at the time. We had owned an old car back when my brothers were at home, but Dad had sold it, since he did not drive. My Dad and Mom usually went to bed at dark to save on the electricity bill. With nothing to do in the country at night, I used a lot of lonely hours literally standing in a window looking up the road for a car light to show atop a hill, thinking that someone might be coming to our house. Sometimes my brother-in-law and sister would come by, and we would go to another family member's house or to a neighborhood friend's house to play Rook, a card game played widely in those days. I was too young to see the mountain that was ahead.

I will instruct thee
and teach thee
in the way
which thou shall go:
I will guide thee
with mine eye.

Psalm 32:8

Chapter Seven
How It All Began

Most of the rural people would go to the nearest town on Saturday to purchase the groceries they were unable to grow and buy other needs for the following week. They would often spend several hours visiting friends and acquaintances on the streets. Sometimes it would be late at night before they would return home. This was the most social activity most of the rural families had during the week, except for Sunday.

The nearest town to the community where we lived was Halls, Tennessee, a small town of approximately two thousand people. Halls "flourished" during the war years, as it was the location of a B-27 Army training base, and even afterward for several years. From North to South, there was two divisional streets, Tigrett and Main. From East to West there were Front Street Highway 51 and College Streets. Halls was a typical agricultural town of the late forties and fifties. All the commerce came from the rural communities surrounding the town. In the fall of the year, when crops were being harvested, it was a busy town. Halls is where my family would go to shop for staples and clothes. Cars, the Internet and other technological advancements, along with the change in routing of Highway 51 have significantly reduced commerce in the town. The town of Halls, Hale's Grocery and the Hale family would change my life.

Hale's Grocery was a small family-owned store started by the older of two sons of this family when he was eighteen years old and with borrowed funds from his uncle, Lonnie Viar. Lonnie Viar was a large landowner and ginner who lived in Halls and owned several hundred acres west of town. The parents of the sons were Raymond F. Hale, Sr., (Mr. Hale) and Pauline (Miss Polly). The boys' names were Raymond, Jr. whom we called "Dub," and later Raymond, and Robert whom we referred to as "Bob." Other employees at various times in the store included Jimmy Moosley, Carl B. Hoggard, Jr. and Jerry Corlew.

Hale's Grocery was located on Front Street. The name was probably given as a result of the street fronting along the Illinois Central Railroad. The depot was diagonally across Front Street from the store. Also across the street between the store and the depot was a large parking strip, and in the forties, it would not be unusual to see a team of mules hitched to a wagon or trailer tied up in the parking strip. The wagon or trailer was used as transportation for the family to go to town for their weekly supplies and social day.

When my parents would go to town to do their shopping and visiting, I found myself hanging around the store. If I may go

Halls Depot and ICC Railroad. (Picture taken in 1991)

back a few years, this started when I was about ten years old. As customers would come in and ask for a particular item, I made it a point to go to the proper shelf and get it for them. Usually the customers would bring in a list that included all the grocery items, and they would give it to Raymond, his brother Bob, Mr. Hale or Miss Polly. The customer would often leave the store and would become a part of the mixture of the street crowd. Their list would be filled and placed in cardboard boxes, which had been saved when groceries had been delivered to the store as inventory. Or the items would go into grass sacks in which potatoes, onions or cabbage had been delivered, or paper bags. We did not offer a choice of paper or plastic. There were no supermarkets where people would come in, choose a basket, and shop for themselves like today.

After some period of time passed, probably two or three years, my unrequested employment continued, Raymond asked me if I would like work all day each Saturday. I was probably either eleven or twelve years old at the time. My elation at this opportunity surely must have been visible. However there was a little problem, in fact, a big problem. The store was open from about 7:30 A.M. until the customers picked up their orders at night, which could be as late as 11:00 P.M. We lived about six miles from town, and I had no transportation. Notwithstanding this, after obtaining permission from my parents, I accepted the opportunity.

The next couple of years presented quite a challenge for me in getting to work each week. Most Saturdays I would get up early, walk about a mile down our gravel road to the community road that was one lane but paved. Sometimes someone would come by and give me a ride to Highway 51 that went to Halls, Dyersburg and others towns North and South. If not, I would walk a couple

Interior of Hale's Grocery. Left to right Bob Hale, Jimmy Moosley, Raymond, Mr. Hale and Lovelace family. (Picture taken about 1947 soon after store was opened)

Exterior of Hale's Grocery. (Picture taken several years later)

Raymond "Dub" and Bob Hale in front of store. Picture taken soon after store opened)

of more miles to the highway and then hitchhike on to Halls. On one occasion I can remember that it was raining, and I promised a neighbor two dollars of my five for the day's work to take me to the store. One day I could not catch a ride and walked the entire six miles. It might be surprising to know that I was waiting on the Hales to open the store that morning.

Sometimes a customer would give me a ride part of the way home at night if convenient. I can remember walking down the gravel road late one winter night in total darkness when I heard footsteps approaching me from the opposite direction. Though I was quite scared, there was nothing to do but keep walking. The person was probably someone I knew in the community. However no words were spoken, and we continued walking, each in our own direction. I shall never forget that night; I have never been more frightened. Raymond or Bob would usually see that I got back home if no ride was available. Later I purchased a bicycle with my earnings and would ride it to work and home at night.

We always had a dog – Jackie, Mickie and later Wimpie – when I was working at the store. Often when I would arrive home late at night Wimpie would hear me as I approached the house down the gravel road. He would bark and make threatening, growling sounds providing the only security we had. However, when I would speak his name, he would recognize my voice and move toward me as if to escort me to safety.

Education was not something my parents believed in. They felt that if you could "figure," calculate your cotton weights, and be able to read and sign your name, that was all the education one needed. They even questioned why I was exerting all my effort and taking risk. I couldn't give them a logical answer.

I had failed in my schoolwork during the fourth grade and was spending the second year in the seventh grade since I was often kept home to work. Most likely I would have dropped out of school except for the fact that you had to be fifteen in those days or you would be reported to the truant officer. My older brothers and sisters had done exactly that – droped out at fifteen – as did their peers. It was the custom in those days for kids with no opportunity.

Why all my determination to get an education? No one will ever know, not even myself. Without a defined goal, each day was a challenge for me. The cliffs in front of me appeared monumental and sometimes would become just that. However, upon reflection, each elevation of a mountain climb is reached one at a time, and without realizing it the plateaus in life were approached and reached in the same manner. Yes, there were some slips, but none were fatal to the climb.

…Love the Lord
and follow His plan
for your lives.
Cling to Him and serve Him
enthusiastically.

Joshua 22:5

Chapter Eight
Leaving Home

My right foot elevated to that first step leading onto the school bus for the last time. As I glanced back toward the old house where now only Mom and Dad would live, a sad feeling engulfed me. All my brothers and sisters were now married with their own families. My sister just two years older had married the previous year, leaving only Mom, Dad and myself. The months since had been lonely, very lonely.

We lived in the country on a gravel road, the last house before the road led into the woods where Pond Creek flowed northward toward to the north fork of the Forked Deer River. We did not have a telephone, nor did my Dad own a car. There was no television, only a radio that was often filled with static to the point everything was difficult to hear. Notwithstanding the static, we sat in front of the radio and listened to baseball games, Amos and Andy, and other programs of the era. Lighting in the homes was not conducive to reading, and if it was, there was no books or other materials. We obviously did not receive a morning paper.

Many nights I would stand by the window that faced the gravel road away from the creek in hopes car lights would appear across the top of the hill about a mile away, perhaps promising a visitor. There was very little traffic since few people in the country owned a car. However when lights did appear, I would watch the car as it moved slowly down the road toward our house. This would be exciting, but then it would move on by our house toward the creek. Night after night this was how my evenings were occupied until the hour became too late for company.

It was November, 1950. This would be my final time to board the bus. A friend, Raymond Hale, Jr., would be coming by the house to get what few clothes I had. He would later come by Hollis Powell Elementary School where I was in the seventh grade to pick me up. Raymond had asked if I would like to come live with them and work in the store in the afternoons and on Saturday and go to school there in town. I can only assume he had discussed this invitation with his family and mine.

There were no domestic problems associated with this move. My parents were very loving but quite poor. They were not excited about the idea of my leaving home, but yielded to my request since it would provide me with an opportunity to stay in school. None of the other children in the family had completed elementary school. If my education was to continue, a change would have to be made.

The move would require me to leave friends I had known and played with for several years. I had been in their homes and spent the night with some of them. Now they would be left behind, and new friendships would have to be made. Yes, children adjust well, but being away from your Mom and Dad, and being surrounded by all the new faces is not exciting to a fourteen-year-old.

The day had arrived that Raymond would pick me up at school and take me to their home. This was not just another day in my life, and it continues to live in my memory as vividly as yesterday. The day was cloudy, cold and dreary. Hardly the type of day that would make anyone excited about leaving home, especially a boy of fourteen. No one of this age could understand what was happening. In fact it would be impossible for anyone to imagine the direction my life was taking and the resulting outcome. Both joy and sadness were inside me and would continue to be for a long time. I had left Mom and Dad alone, and I was lonely for them. I felt like someone other than myself had taken control of my life.

Needless to say, my clothing was not in keeping with that of the other children that I became associated with in school. My high top shoes were quite different from the loafers and tennis shoes being worn by the other children. The "sawmill" socks were not exactly a fashion symbol.

My entrance into a town school also proved that I was not as prepared as the other students. They were more advanced in every subject. Perhaps most of my problems were with English where I struggled in both writing and speaking correctly. Some of the students had been in school together for seven years, and to be accepted as a part of this group was not easy.

Hale's House. (Picture Taken Several Years Later)

Living with the Hales became a challenge. At some point Raymond shared with me that since he and Bob would both be in college, he wanted me to be with his mother. It subsequently became known that Mr. Hale had left the family in prior years for some period of time and had returned only a few years before I became associated with them. He wanted me there to be sure his mother was not abused.

This presented a little problem, as Mr. Hale appeared to resent my being there. As a result he often would say or do something that would hurt me deeply and send me to bed crying. He expected me to use different soap and hand towel from that used by the family. Perhaps I was just too sensitive. However, it should be remembered that my age was fourteen, and I was struggling with being away from home and in a totally new environment. I often wondered how I could continue and what direction my life would take next. Once at the store, when I had an accident and broke a jar of pickles, Mr. Hale became upset and told me that if it ever happened again he would take the cost out of my earnings. Obviously, I tried to be more careful.

Miss Polly was a very kind and gracious lady and did everything she could for me to feel comfortable. She treated me as if I was one of her sons. She worked hard in the store as well as the home. She never indicated that it bothered her that she was cooking for an additional person or washing my clothes. In appreciation of her attitude toward me, I tried to do everything possible to eliminate her workload at the store and to help her at home with any chore that I could find, including the dishes.

The year and a half that I lived with the Hales proved to be difficult at times, but we made it. My peers at school had accepted me, and the teachers appeared to realize my difficulties and take a special interest in me. Fortunately I had an excellent English grammar teacher who made sure that we understood proper sentence structure. It was necessary that a little work be done on a sentence-diagramming workbook during the summer, but the eight grade was completed.

Mr. And Mrs. Hale. (Picture, courtesy of Olan Mills, taken about 1952)

While living with the Hales I came to know James and Mary Ann Peery who lived next door in a duplex owned by the Hales. Mr. Peery was coach during the time I lived with the Hales and would become principal of the high school. Mrs. Peery taught algebra and geometry at the high school. When I lived with the Hales, I called Mr. Peery, "Jim" and Mrs. Peery, "Mary Ann." I didn't slip up too many times when I got to high school. Mr. Peery became a significant person in my life.

God said, "I will never fail you.
I will never forsake you."

Hebrews 13:5

Chapter Nine
My Greatest Challenge

My work at the store continued throughout the following year. However, during the summer of 1952 both Hale sons were married. Raymond told me that I could continue working at the store as long as I cared to, but that since he and Bob were married there would not be room in their home for me any longer, as there would not be a bedroom available when they came home. This appeared to be the end of my education, as I had no place to go but back to the country. This was devastating. I had sacrificed so much and worked so hard, and now it appeared as if there were no alternatives left for me.

There was a boarding house in town, a large home occupied primarily by transient people. Originally it had been constructed as a hotel and had served as such during the war. In fact, it was known as the Massengill Hotel. Mrs. Mary Perry and her husband Bill owned the boarding house and lived there themselves. They are not to be confused with the Peerys.

High school was to commence on Monday, and I wasn't sure on this particular Saturday whether or not I would be able to attend. I did not know Mrs. Perry personally but had seen her around town. In addition to running the boarding house, she held a part time job at Levy's Department Store. Something inside urged me to go down that afternoon and talk with her. By this time many people in town knew of the sacrifices that I was making and my effort to stay in school. I got permission to leave the store and went to visit with Mrs. Perry about my situation.

When I stepped up on the porch toward the door I could see her resting on the bed in one of the front bedrooms. My immediate thoughts were that the timing was bad; she had been disturbed and perhaps would be in a bad mood. This could lead to her total rejection. She sat up on the bed for a minute and then gracefully approached the door. When the door was opened we stood exchanging greeting, and I gave her an introduction of myself and made the request to talk with her more privately.

Mrs. Perry was a gracious lady, and I later learned that she had taken in other boys who, for one reason or another, had come to her seeking a place to stay. We had a short visit in which I explained my situation to her. I shared with her that I had been living and working with the Hales. I told her my employment at the store could continue, but that they would no longer have room for me in their home. She took time to show me around the house. In the tour she took me to a small room located on the second floor on the front of the house. The room contained a half bed (a bed for one person), and one chair. The room had a wire extended across one side and a cloth curtain hung on it. This was the closet. When we had returned downstairs she said that I could have the small room she had shown me and two meals a day for eight dollars a week. My salary at the store working afternoons after school and all day on Saturday would be twelve dollars. This would give me four dollars for other needs.

There was really no choice for me. I had no other alternative and nothing to loose. If it worked out that would be great; if not, I could rethink my position. Her offer was accepted. My recall does not include any discussions with my parents or what their thoughts were about my decision. At this point I had lived away from home almost two years and had been somewhat on my own as far as my parents were concerned. My dad really had no money, so he had been unable to contribute to my needs. It was probably difficult for them to understand why I made all the sacrifices, since they had no appreciation for an education. While

I was only fifteen years old, my Dad must have had faith in me, as he did not attempt to direct my life.

Without question God had been working in my life for several years, and He continued to guide me up the mountain before me. There is no other explanation how a kid my age, with no help from his parents could be in the position that I found myself.

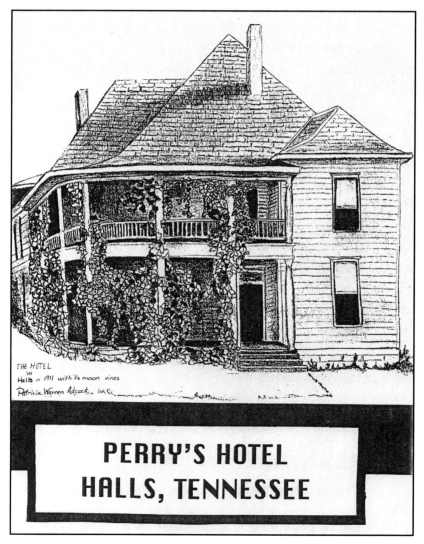

Perry's Hotel. Drawing ©Patricia Warren Adcock, used with permission.

While my parents were too poor to provide financial assistance, what they did provide were morals and ethics that would see me through many trials. Such expressions as, "Watch the company you keep," and "Don't forget your raising" often made my decision about a choice that came before me.

A small town has its advantages and disadvantages. In my situation the advantages led the way. Working at the store and delivering groceries on a bicycle had carried me all over town and into many of the homes of the townspeople. The people knew me, and most of them knew my background, the sacrifices that I was making and my desire to go to school.

School began and sure enough the freshman class included me. There were one hundred ten of us that year, and sixty-eight would continue on to graduation. Mrs. Perry would make sure that I was up in time to come down stairs and have breakfast at the boarding house table with everyone else and get to school on time. She was instrumental in changing the direction of my life, and I will never forget what she did for me. I was very fortunate to have three mothers, my own mother, Mrs. Hale and Mrs. Perry.

Soon after our classes commenced, Mr. Peery, the principal who had lived next door to the Hales, called me in to his office. He obviously knew my needs and my economic situation and wanted to be sure I had the proper food to eat. As a result he provided me with a meal ticket that entitled me to eat in the cafeteria at school free. This was a tremendous help, as it would not take part of my earnings from the store. I later learned that he, too, had to struggle to get through college, and he was expressing his empathy in this way.

Being away from home so young was not always easy. My emotions would sometimes be more than I could accept. The events that were occurring in my life were simply unexplainable. There was no way to understand what was transpiring. The element of depression was never a problem, but self-pity, sadness and feeling sorry for myself often slept with me as I closed my eyes some nights.

I made sure to do all my homework in the evenings after work, and my grades were good. My work in the afternoons at the store made it hard for me to participate in sporting event. However, I did play freshman football and made the varsity basketball team. I would usually go home on Saturday night and spend Sunday with my family. These were challenging times for me but would prove to be the type of foundation needed for the higher elevations that were ahead.

Late one Saturday night during this freshman year, Mr. Hale called me back behind the meat counter at the store. He proceeded to tell me that they would have to cut my pay at the store. This presented a real problem for me, as there was no way that I could go forward with anything less than I was making. Harry Lee Rhodes who owned the drug store was already permitting me to purchase items on credit until I could work in the summer and pay him back. Louis Levy who owned the department store was also extending credit for my essential clothing needs. How could I live with anything less? I became quite emotional and could not hold back the tears. When Raymond saw me crying he came back and asked me, "What is the problem?" After composing myself a bit I related to him what his dad had told me. He said, "Your salary is not going to be reduced. Don't let what he said bother you." In the months after that, Raymond would always make sure that I received something more rather than less.

That first year in high school was a great challenge. I was just excited to be with my friends and complete the year of high school. At that point I had achieved more education than anyone else in my entire family. After the school year was over I moved back to the country to work on the farm but maintained my work at the store on Saturdays. Often I would go to town on Friday afternoon, work a few hours at the store, spend the night with friends, and be available to work the next day. There was a youth center in town that included a skating rink, and it was always good to go there on Friday nights and see everyone.

During the summer between my freshman and sophomore years, one of my brothers and his wife moved to town. He told me that if I could get me some type of bed I could live with them the next school year. A roll away bed, one that could be folded up and rolled out of the way, was purchased, and when school started, I moved in with them. As I recall they did not charge me anything for living with them so this was a big improvement over the previous year.

My sophomore year was somewhat uneventful. Work continued at the store after school and on Saturdays. I played basketball but did not go out for the varsity football team, as I was afraid of being injured. That would have been devastating.

Life was a little easier during this period of time; at least it appeared to be. My parents moved to Halls the summer prior to my junior year in high school. There was an agreement arranged with my parents that I would pay the house rent if they could manage the other expenses. The rent was only $30.00 per month, and I had paid more than that my freshman year at the boarding house. My Dad and Mother would pick up odd jobs to pay the other bills. I had a sister who had lost her husband, and she and two children also lived with us during this period of time. I should give her credit here for assisting with the expenses. This was a tremendous help to me. I could live at home, be with my family and stay in school. One of my brother-in-laws had let me use his car to get my driver's license during that summer. However, Mr. Hale would not permit me use the truck for the delivery of groceries as was the custom. This required me to continue making deliveries on the bike until I was nineteen years of age.

Sports became a big part of my life and we had championship teams in both basketball and football. The girls' teams during these years were also exceptional. I was elected class president during my junior year, and this was good for me. Being elected class president gave me a lot of confidence. A class was taught in those days called Distributive Education, and my class decided to nominate me to run for state president, which I won. There were some strong political contacts in this election for it to be at the high school level. My campaign manager's name was Martha Clayton. This name will surface later as she would become an important part of my life.

These days we hear that God winks, and this was truly a "God wink" for me. Distributive Education was a class that was offered to those students who were working while attending school. The grade was awarded in part by the school and in part by the employer. Another honor was given me by the townspeople. The American Legion Post chose me to attend Boy's State. Boys State was a week long, expense-free, event where various civic organizations would sponsor a boy to attend and learn about state government. It was quite an honor to be selected as the outstanding young male high school student and be invited to attend Boy's State.

One of the things that I liked to do was to caddy some Sunday afternoons for a couple of golfers who lived in town. L. R. Viar, who owned the Ford Dealership in town, was one of these people. I also mowed his lawn on Wednesday afternoons when the store was closed. Closing on Wednesday was a practice of all the stores in town during the summer months.

Class rings were always ordered during the junior year in school. In those days high school class rings only cost $19. While this may not appear to be much money today, it was almost two weeks' work at the store and over one half month's rent. It was more than I had, and my parents could not afford to buy me a ring. When it came time to order the class rings, I went to L. R. to borrow the money. I knew he would afford me this request. Contrary to my thoughts he turned me down. Notwithstanding this, late in his life, I had the opportunity to show him and his wife Mary Walker some courtesies as we lived near each other in Memphis at the time of his death. His dad was the same person who had loaned Raymond the money to open the grocery store. I went to see Mr. Lonnie and told him my situation, and he immediately wrote me a check for the amount. He was later repaid.

In the spring of my junior year in high school, Mr. Peery, the principal of the high school wrote these words in my yearbook. "Bill, life sometimes is hard to deal with. You deserve a commendation for your efforts. You have done a wonderful job in school, on the athletic fields and floors, and at home. Best of Luck. Keep working."

My senior year was exciting and exceptional. It was an outstanding year. My grades were good, and many honors were bestowed upon me. Class President, Honor Student, Most Courteous, Best All Around, Friendliest, and Most Outstanding Football Player were some of the honors won during my senior year. It was almost impossible to believe that these honors were being awarded to the same boy who moved to town from the country.

Was this the same person who had experienced problems being accepted into the class five and one-half years earlier? My parents probably did not realize the importance of all the honors I had been given in school. The Hales were pleased with my achievements, and I know they felt like they had been a part of the reason why I was given the honors. They should have been; they were. If ever I was conceited it was at this point in my life. I was proud of my accomplishments in life and in school. Our class excelled in the classroom, on the basketball court and football field.

How could someone like me, with poor grammar, few clothes and no financial support from my parents, move into town as a seventh grader and win the trust and friendship of so many people. The entire series of events that had occurred in my life were almost frightening.

Raymond Hale, Jr. had completed his college and was in the Air Force. Raymond continued to communicate with me and told me some day he would have a big super market and he wanted me to work with him. This made me feel good for several reasons. One, it told me that he was pleased with my work at the store and with me. Secondly, he had been fair in every way and my future was lacking in direction. I had learned the grocery business and enjoyed it. An opportunity to work with him in a super market would have been great for me.

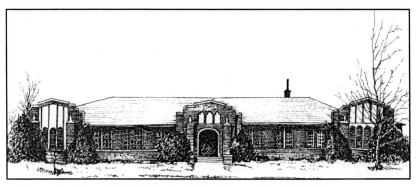

Reproduction of High School. (School burned in 1980's)

UNITED STATES AIR FORCES

Sunday

Dear Bill,

How's everything going with you Bill? I guess it gets pretty hot for you on Wednesday when you are cutting yards. You make all the money you can because I'll want to borrow some in a couple of years.

I'm going to appoint you as the number one official to look after Mom & Dad and to take care of business at the store. Some day you & I will have a big super-market and you can be my manager and right hand man.

Bob's going to be stationed about a hundred miles away from me so I'll be seeing lots of him.

I won't have much work to do at the base. Nobody works too hard in the Air Force.

Daddy said you all were working on Jim Peeny's house. Don't let Daddy get you too hot.

Tell everybody hello & I'll be seeing you soon.

your buddy.

"Dub"

Raymond's letter when he was in the Air Force

I can do all things through
Christ who gives me strength.

Philippians 4:13

Chapter Ten
A Plateau Was Reached

Graduation from high school was a happy time for me, but also a very sad time. Accomplishments that I had never dreamed of had been achieved, and yet the thought of separating from this group of friends was difficult. We had been so close and now everyone would be going his or her separate way. This would be the end of my work at Hale's Grocery. I had been around the store now for almost ten years, and it wasn't easy to leave, yet the store promised no future for me.

Somewhere along the way I had set as a goal for myself to obtain a college degree. This was a lofty dream, but one that possibly was achievable. My athletic skills had awarded me with a one-half scholarship in football at Murray State College in Kentucky. As a matter of information, of the eleven seniors on our football team of eithteen, four of us received football scholarships, one to Vanderbilt, one to Memphis State College, and two to Murray State College. In the fall, about four weeks before school was to commence, I reported to the coach at Murray State. After several days of practice, conversation with the coach suggested that a full scholorship would not be available. Upon learning this, I came home and enrolled at Memphis State College. My thoughts were that I could work and go to school.

After enrolling in school my next objective was to get a job to support myself. The only thing I had done, except for farm labor, was to work in a grocery store. It was natural that my occupation became a checker in a large Memphis supermarket known as Foodtown at the corner of Highland and Summer. This was a large store for its time, having ten cash registers at the front. This experience was quite different from Hale's Grocery where we added the merchandise up on a Victor adding machine.

Late one Saturday evening, after I was off work, I decided to hitchhike home to see my parents. I was able to catch a ride out to a town about 35 miles north of Memphis called Munford. It was in the fall of the year and the night temperatures could decrease to the 30's. The traffic almost ceased and I was stranded. As the temperature dropped and my chances of a ride diminished, I found shelter in an outside bathroom of a service station. Somewhere near midnight two black men arrived outside the door. As they talked I became frightened since there was no way for me to lock the door. At that point I sat down in the floor of the bathroom, placing my back against the wall and my feet against the door. After some time had elapsed the men made an attempt to enter the bathroom. They pushed and shoved but were unsuccessful in opening the door. After a few attempts they left.

The next morning the station owner arrived, opened the station, and I shared my experience with him. He made me welcome and insisted that I remain until I had become comfortable

Service station. The restroom is partially visible near the back of the building. (Picture taken several years later)

from the night's cold. Later I was able to catch a ride on to my parents home. The old station remains. However, it is now used as some retail store.

Sonny Higdon, one of my high school classmates had also enrolled at Memphis State. We had played basketball and football together, and he had worked at a small grocery store/meat market during high school. Sonny and I shared a garage apartment off campus, and I worked in a grocery store after classes and on Saturdays. Since I did not have a car it was necessary that I hitchhike or catch a city bus to work and back home. It was not the perfect situation. Sonny was instrumental in my getting a job at Barnwell-Hays Cotton Company where he was working, and this helped as Sonny had a car, and I could ride with him to work and back home. Several hours of work were needed to make sure my expenses were paid. Unfortunately the more hours I worked, the less time I had for studies. I kept this up for two semesters. However my grades suffered, and I was unable to enroll the third semester.

After dropping out one semester I tried again. Bob Hale and his wife were now living in Memphis, and he invited me to live with them during this semester. They lived quite a distance from the college, and it became very difficult for me to get back and forth to school and to work. With real intentions and a great desire to continue in school, my limited financial resources simply would not permit it. After one semester I had to drop out.

It was July, the year was 1958, and I was twenty-one years of age. The Army was beginning to express some interest in me. Said differently, in those days there was a draft in effect, and if you were not in school, you were quite vulnerable to being drafted into service. Without employment and no desire to be drafted into the Army, I chose to volunteer for three years so that I might be more selective in my military career.

James Davis, a friend I had known from Bruceville who had attended the University of Tennessee at Martin for a couple of years, and I went into service together. We took our basic training at Fort Chaffee, Arkansas, and went to Fort Eustis, Virginia, to a specialized aviation training school that lasted twenty-three weeks. Most of the graduates of the school, including James, were being sent to Korea at that particular time to work on helicopters. My parents were elderly, and I did not want to leave the country for Korea. Some weeks before graduation, I approached the Captain in the school to see what the chances were for me to remain in the school as an instructor. He was receptive to my request and when the orders came down at the end of school, I was appointed to the training school. Fortunately for me, I remained there for the balance of my career.

The years in service proved to be very beneficial. Discipline as I had never known it was instilled in me, and while I had been managing on my own for several years, I learned that there was only one paycheck each month. There would always be a bunk and food in the mess hall. However, if you spent your paycheck you had to wait a long time for another one.

After attending an instructional school for four weeks, I was then ready for the classroom. This was a great experience for me. I had taken public speaking in college, and the course was very valuable. My workday consisted of writing lesson plans and teaching two or three courses a day. Soon I had arranged my classes where they could be taught in the mornings and early afternoon, and I was free after that. I was able to obtain a job in a grocery story in Williamsburg, Virginia. This was only eight miles from the post. The job permitted me to buy my first car, a used 1957 Ford. I was now twenty-three years old and finally had my own transportation.

Needless to say I had made a lot of friends around the post and in Williamsburg. Army life was a great experience and helped me cope in the years that followed. While in service I met John Applegate, who became one of my closest friends. John was from New Jersey just across the Hudson River from New York City. On several occasions John would invite me to go home with him and spend the weekend. John was discharged a couple of months before me and he returned to New Jersey. John later asked me to be the best man at his wedding.

There was an opportunity for me to continue working at the military post as a civilian instructor, doing basically the same work that I had been doing. This was a very attractive option. However, Martha Clayton who was mentioned earlier, and I had maintained an on-and-off relationship. Martha had obtained a degree in secondary education and was teaching in Memphis. Perhaps my relationship with her, more than anything else, made my decision not to stay in Virginia.

The Family (1959) Left to right (back row) James, Oscar (Dad), Charles, B.W., Bill (self), Onzie (front row) Pokie (Mom), Bessie, Emma Jean, Marie, Mae

No eye has seen,
no ear has heard,
and no mind has imagined
what God has prepared
for those who love him.

1 Corinthians 2:9

Chapter Eleven
The Summit

During these years I had maintained conversation with the Hales and particularly Raymond. After college and his military career, Raymond moved to Chattanooga and opened a real estate sales office. He later established an insurance company and invited his brother Bob to join him in the business. Raymond also entered the home building business. Mr. and Mrs. Hale had sold the store in Halls and had moved to Chattanooga also. Mr. Hale handled the home building business for Raymond.

Upon my discharge from the Army, Raymond offered me an opportunity to move to Chattanooga and work with him in the real estate sales business. This would be a completely new field for me, and I knew nothing about real estate. There were not many opportunities for me, so I accepted Raymond's offer. I joined the firm of Hale Realty Company as a sales person in August, 1961. Raymond paid me a salary to assist him with odd jobs around the office until I could obtain a sales license and sell real estate on a commission basis. I studied hard, took a course in real estate at the University of Chattanooga and was able to pass my exam and obtain my license within a three-months period of time.

A successful real estate sales person had to work long hours. We often worked six days a week in the office and then would hold open house in a home or subdivision on Sunday afternoon. Since I was so new and had no referral business, I had to work even harder.

On July 20, 1962, Martha Clayton and I were married in Jackson, Tennessee. We have now enjoyed more than 45 years together. Her father, a Methodist minister, blessed our marriage and performed the ceremony. Our families were quite different, and this gave me some concern prior to our marriage and immediately thereafter. Her family was all educated with degrees, and my family was quite the opposite. Many of her relatives were ministers in the Methodist denomination. Although my family were people of deep faith, they were not as close to the church as they should have been. The Claytons accepted me, a Baptist and without a college degree, into the family, and there were absolutely no problems.

Martha was able to obtain a position with the Chattanooga School System, and my sales work was progressing. We were able to build us a home and soon sold it for a profit. Everything was going well, and we later built another home for ourselves. All this time I was thinking of my dream to obtain a college degree. However, the hours that I was working would not permit me to go back to college. Much like many previous times, a new opportunity presented itself. In 1966, after working for Raymond for five years, I had an opportunity to go to work with Interstate Life and Accident Insurance Company in their real estate investment department. It was a difficult decision to leave Raymond since he had been so good to me all my life. However, something urged me onward and the decision became a monumental one for me.

Insurance premiums that were obtained from policies issued were invested in different areas, and real estate was one form of the company's areas of investment. My real estate experience at Hale Realty had assisted in my obtaining this position. The responsibility assigned to me would be to audit single-family residential files and then prepare vouchers for payment back to the originators of the loans, our correspondents. I would also assist in the balance of the real estate records each month.

Interstate was located almost directly across the street from the University of Chattanooga. In my new position I could enroll in the evening college and work on my degree. Executive management at Interstate was great. They were very much interested in their employees and had a program to pay for classes

Interstate Life & accident insurance company

HOME OFFICE • CHATTANOOGA, TENNESSEE

Serving and protecting millions since 1909

H. CLAY EVANS JOHNSON
President

February 10, 1967

Dear Bill,

    This is your first compensation check from the Interstate Life & Accident Insurance Company, and with it I want to extend our welcome to you as a new member of our organization.

    If you have not already done so, you will find that the over 350 men and women who compose the personnel of the Home Office are an enthusiastic, energetic and interested group of people who take seriously the responsibility of their duties in connection with furnishing insurance coverage and service in the Southern states in which we operate.

    We want your association with this Company to be as pleasant and interesting as it can be made, and your selection by us as a new employee was made upon our belief that you are the type of person who can fit in and work with those of us who are already employed here. The Interstate is really the result of the combined actions of all its employees, carrying out their various duties. Thus, your contacts with our policyholders and the public in the discharge of your duties make an impression upon them, either good or bad, which is reflected upon all of us.

    If at any time you are asked questions concerning the operations of the Company with which you are not familiar, your supervisor or I will be glad to give you the necessary information. You should familiarize yourself with the entire operations of the Company as much as possible, in addition to the duties of the position which you occupy. Our policy, where advisable and possible, is to promote our own employees to our more responsible and remunerative positions.

    Again I want to extend to you a welcome into our organization, whose work I believe you will find most interesting.

Sincerely,

H. C. E. JOHNSON

HCEJ:gk

LIFE • HEALTH & ACCIDENT • FIRE

Letter from Interstate Life Insurance Company, H. C. E. Johnson, President that would benefit them in their work. My tuition was being paid by benefits of the Veterans Administration, but Interstate would also issue me a check each time I had received a passing grade for a course. If I was unable to schedule a class that I needed in the evenings, they would give me time off during the day. What a great bunch of people. What a great company. The chairman of the board knew everyone by name and spoke to them by name. I later learned this was the exception rather than the rule in the business world.

When I was trying to enroll at the University of Chatta-nooga, the lady in admissions looked at my transcript from Memphis State College and told me that I was not college material. She told me only my high entrance exam scores permitted my entrance. After going to school four nights a week for five years I earned a BS in Business Administration. The University of Chattanooga had joined the University of Tennessee system and became known as University of Tennessee at Chattanooga. Raymond and his wife, Ann, attended the graduation ceremony. After graduating I went back to the admissions office, took a copy of my transcript and had a little meeting with the lady that had been so unkind to me five years earlier. We got everything worked out, and I doubt that she would ever be so rude again. She simply had not understood my struggles in trying to get an education.

My goal in life had been achieved. I had graduated from College. I could not help but reminisce over the direction my life had taken: the hard days at the store, leaving home and moving in with the Hales and the challenges that were presented, my living in the boarding house, and my high school years. Truly some power stronger than my own desire had made all this possible.

One of the first things I did was to sit down and write Mrs. Perry, the lady at the boarding house, a long letter. In the letter I told her that nineteen years earlier she had made available to me

Mrs. Hale, Raymond "Dub" and Bob. Picture taken in 1965

a small room and two meals a day. In doing this she had given me an opportunity to stay in school and now after graduation from college, I wanted to thank her once again. I visited her many times in a nursing home in her last years, always taking presents and flowers in appreciation of what she did for me.

While I was in college my responsibilities at Interstate changed significantly. The spread in interest rates between single-family mortgages and commercial mortgages caused us to change the mix in our real estate investment portfolio. This gave me an opportunity to move into commercial mortgages and underwriting of large real estate loans. The experience gained here would prove to be the foundation of my future.

Soon after I received my degree, Interstate Life and Accident Insurance Company gave me a significant salary increase. My immediate boss, Bob Collins, and Carl Arnold, the treasurer of the company, were elated at my achievements. They often talked with me about my future with Interstate, and Mr. Arnold once asked for permission to come to our home and talk with Martha and me. They were afraid that I would leave the company.

While I was in college, Martha had become pregnant on more than one occasion but had not been successful in carrying the baby to maturity. After several unsuccessful attempts of having a child born to us, we chose adoption. In March, 1970, we adopted a beautiful, five weeks old boy whom we named Scot Clayton McLaughlin. In June of the following year we had a daughter born to us whom we named Kimberly Dawn McLaughlin

Martha terminated her employment at school when we adopted Scot. However, I was doing well at Interstate, and we could live comfortably without her income. God had been good to us. One of my older sisters came to visit us in Chattanooga, and when she saw our home and the view of the mountains from our front yard she said to me, "Don't you just have to pinch yourself to believe this?" I could now see the peak of the mountaintop.

In 1972 both of Martha's parents died within a relatively short period of time. All of our relatives were in West Tennessee, and we were able to visit infrequently. We valued our family relationships and discussed the possibility of moving to Memphis so that we could be closer to them. In the summer I sent out resumes to some companies in Memphis and in a short period of time had accepted a job with James E. McGehee and Company, a mortgage company that was owned by National Bank of Commerce. We not only had an opportunity to move back to West Tennessee but also had our moving expenses paid. In addition, I received a sizeable promotion, new car with an open credit card.

Notwithstanding the challenge of a new job and courtesies afforded me, the decision was a difficult one for us. When I had accepted this position and told my superiors at Interstate Life of my decision to move, they were perplexed. They did everything they could to keep me. Mr. Arnold, the treasurer would make it a point to spend some time with me to see if anything could be worked out. The ironic thing about all this was the fact that within three years after I left Interstate, the company was sold to Gulf Life Insurance Company in Jacksonville, Florida, and the employees either moved to Jacksonville or found other places of employment in Chattanooga.

Martha, the children and I moved into a comfortable new home in the Balmoral section of East Memphis. My employment with the new company went well. My responsibility was to originate commercial real estate loans that could be purchased by life insurance companies for their investment portfolios. I found myself on the opposite side of the fence from what I had been doing with Interstate. The position provided me an opportunity to learn a different side of the business.

On each origination the life insurance companies required an appraisal of the property. After taking several real estate appraisal courses, I was able to complete the appraisal myself along with the submission of the loan package for approval by the life companies we represented. This eventually led to my obtaining a real estate appraisal designation through the Society of Real Estate Appraisers, a nationally recognized appraisal organization. The Society has now merged with the Institute of Real Estate Appraisers and there is only the one organization called the Institute. The time with this company was very rewarding and permitted Martha and me to attend national conventions and visit many cities to include San Francisco, Boston, Chicago and New York.

In 1975 I was promoted to Vice President of James E. McGehee and Company. My career now appeared secure. The following year we sold our home in Balmoral and built a home in Germantown. This move was necessitated due to the busing issue. There was a community school in Balmoral. However, our children would have had to be bussed several miles to an intercity school. Choosing not to permit this type of nonsense, we moved so that the children would be included in the Shelby County school system.

One Saturday in 1980, while Martha and I were having a sandwich for lunch, I received a telephone call from Jim Gurley. Jim was at the time Senior Vice President and head of the real estate division of Union Planters Bank. Someone had given him my name as a possibility for a position he had open. He asked me if I would be interested in coming in to talk with him about the position. This is not the normal pattern of how one obtains a position with a bank or how a position is filled. However, given the directions my life had taken, perhaps it was all in the plan.

I agreed to go in and meet with Jim and discuss the position that was available. Union Planters had been the largest bank in Memphis at one time and was considered as an excellent place to work during those days. As a result of some fraudulent transactions in the real estate division, prior to the time that Jim was assigned to the area, Union Planters had lost its market position. In truth, the bank was almost closed by regulators in the mid-seventies due to the non-performing real estate loans and the bank's financial position. The bank had $200 million in non-earning assets, largely real estate. My visit with Jim and later with Rudy Holmes, Jim's superior, went well, and I became employed by the bank as a vice president on June 18, 1980.

Within three years after I had left James E. McGehee & Company, the National Bank of Commerce sold the company to Polk Mortgage Company in North Carolina. After a short period of time the loans were moved to their home office and the entire staff was dismissed. Was this providence? How does one explain things like this that happen in life – not once but twice? I can only think that someone engineered the plan of my life other than myself.

Union Planters
NATIONAL BANK OF MEMPHIS
Post Office Box 387 • Memphis, TN 38147

June 9, 1980

Mr. Billy R. McLaughlin
2505 Cedarwood Drive
Germantown, TN   38138

Dear Mr. McLaughlin:

Thank you for the time you spent with us discussing employment opportunities with Union Planters National Bank.

This is to confirm to you our offer of employment. Your
position will be Manager, Commercial Mortgage Underwriting,
effective June 16, 1980, conditional upon the successful
passing of physical and fingerprinting examinations.

Your starting salary will be $30,000.00 per annum. Pending
approval of the Board of Directors, you will be given the
official title of Vice President.

The enclosed schedule lists those benefits which the Bank
offers. Included in this schedule are the eligibility require-
ments for each benefit. We will be happy to discuss any
questions you may have.

We are most happy to bring you aboard and wish you a very
successful career at Union Planters.

Sincerely,

M. Kirk Walters
Senior Vice President
Director of Personnel

/lf

Letter from Kirk Walters, Sr. V. P. and Director of Personnel, Union Planters National Bank

For the first ten years at the bank I worked on problem real estate loans that were remaining from the seventies. The portfolio consisted of hotels, apartments, medical buildings and condos. Some of the properties would be sold two or three times before we could get paid off on the loans. There was litigation going on all the time. One of the most stressful times of my life was when a lawsuit was filed against the bank for lender liability on a hotel loan in Laredo, Texas. The lawsuit was in the amount of four hundred million dollars, and I was the only officer representing the bank. The trial lasted almost two weeks before a settlement was reached, and I was much relieved. Dealing with bankruptcies and foreclosures were a part of the daily routine.

In the mid-eighties, Bill Matthews, the Chairman who had been brought into the bank to turn it around in the seventies, had become quite aggressive, and the bank entered into a loan program that again led to near disaster. He was dismissed, and Ben Rawlins was brought in as the new CEO. In the early nineties the bank began to break out of the problems of the seventies and mid-eighties. Most of the loans had been managed to the point that they were performing satisfactorily. The bank was in a better financial position, and Mr. Rawlins commenced an aggressive acquisition program.

In 1990 I was promoted to Senior Vice President and named manager of the real estate division. This responsibility included the production and management of both single family and commercial real estate loans. I held this position until 1996 when a lot of people were moved around as a result of a large in-market acquisition. Mr. Rawlins arranged with Edgar Bailey, CEO of Leader Enterprises, Inc., the purchase of that company. It was a large savings and loan association in Memphis. Unfortunately for Union Planters' employees, everyone, including myself, was displaced to make room for Leader Federal employees. Apparently this was a part of the negotiated deal.

I was moved out of the real estate lending function into special assets. In this position I was responsible for managing the bank's foreclosed properties and doing special assignments. This was not a pleasant assignment to accept. However during the climb, I had learned that some lateral and backward motion was required to move upward.

HALE REALTY

7540 EAST BRAINERD ROAD
CHATTANOOGA, TENNESSEE 37421
PHONE (615) 894-4763

REALTOR®

June 18, 1991

Bill McLaughlin
Senior Vice President
Union Planters National Bank
P. O. Box 387
Memphis, TN 38147

Dear Bill:

Congratulations on the excellent turn out you had for your class reunion.
Jim Peery said it was one of the best he has attended. He said you did an
outstanding job as MC, and he complimented you very much. I want to tell you
how proud I am of what you have accomplished since working at Hales' Grocery!
You are one of the ones that I consider a self-made man. You have accomplished
very much in life and I know Martha has been a great help to you.

I want to thank you for putting me in touch with Joe Holt and the listing I
have at 311 South Palisades Drive. Last week I talked with Evelyn Amedo and
she will be handling this listing as well as 3 condos that you have on
Pleasant Run Road here in Chattanooga.

We are all doing fine. Ann and I spent a week in Daytona Beach last month
and enjoyed it very much. Bob Hale had a hip replacement and was in the
hospital one week. He is recovering well and will have the other operated on
in a couple of months.

Come to see us in Chattanooga when you can. Thanks again for the good business
you are favoring me with. Best regards to Martha, Kim, and Scott.

Sincerely,

Dub

RH/sc

Enclosure

"For A Quick Sale -- Call HALE"

Letter received from Raymond "Dub" in 1991

On January 1, 1999, I was promoted from the Memphis
Bank to the corporate offices to become the Senior Real Estate
Credit Officer for Union Planters Corporation, a company that
is the largest Tennessee chartered bank with assets in excess of
38 billion dollars. My responsibilities in this position included

underwriting and approval of real estate loans in excess of 20 million dollars and writing real estate policy and procedures for the bank. I maintained that position until retirement.

Current Home (2007)

My Family in 2007. From left are Bill, Martha, Scot and Kim.

Thanks.

Chapter Twelve
The Valley Lies Ahead

A lot of time has been covered in the previous chapters, and a lot has been said. Nothing that has been written is intended to be egotistical, but only that God has been good to me in many ways. For everything good, I give Him the credit. I accept the responsibility for the bad. He has placed many people in my life's path and has been my guide up life's mountain.

God sent me Martha and gave to us two great children. We were able to guide them through many temptations in life that many young people succumb to today. We were able to provide each of them an education in the university of their choice, and each of them has responsible, productive sources of employment. Our daughter, Kim, lives in Bartlett, Tennessee, and works for Pfizer Pharmaceutical Company as a staff accountant in the Financial Division. She and Chris, her husband, have provided us with two granddaughters, Layton and Mabry. Our son, Scot, lives in Nashville, Tennessee, and is an officer with Regions Bank. He is not married as this book is completed.

Yes, if I had an opportunity, I would do some things differently. However, we don't have yesterday, only tomorrow. Accordingly, we must use our time remaining in accordance with His plan for our lives.

Through life there have been many expressions by those whom I have met and who have known me. With fear of being considered boastful, I would like to relate some of what people have told me.

Mrs. Travis Davis, the secretary to the principal of the high school told me on a return visit to Halls, "Billy, you do not know how many lives you have touched in this town." This is one of the greatest compliments in my life.

Mr. Charles Viar, when introduced to my wife forty years after I graduated from high school, told her, "I don't know where you found him. My wife and I never had any children, but if a son had been born to us, I would have wanted him to be just like Billy."

Raymond Hale wrote in a letter received several years ago, "You have accomplished much in life since you worked at the store. I consider you as a self made man."

Mrs. Audrey Braden, a member of my Sunday school class, said, "Rudyard Kipling must have had you in mind when he penned the poem *If*."

These and other expressions have sustained me through life. Yes, there have been some things happen in my life that I am not proud of. God has promised to forgive these, and I believe He will.

The retirement years are upon me, and I know there will be other challenges. As I enjoy the fruits of the valley, I will look back at the mountain and remember each plateau. With God as my guide and the help of others, I made it over the top. I have kept my faith, and the rewards in life have been greater than any dream could have provided. The beautiful valley is now before me.

In looking back over the years I would like to think that I started at the bottom and ended up at the bottom. While I consider my life as being quite successful, given the humble beginnings, my roots are still there. Bruceville, Halls, Hale's Grocery, Halls High School and all those who assisted me in my climb will always be the subject of my favorite thoughts.

Goudy and Berylium on LSI 55# creme white
Type and design by Karen Stone

Printed in the United States
203854BV00001BD/82-96/P

9 780981 499673